Old MAYBOLE & NORTH CARRICK

by
Susan Milligan

As the town of Maybole grew it followed its water supply. The early town was at the foot of a south-facing slope to take advantage of the water supply from the burns and springs flowing downhill. Later the springs on slightly higher ground were opened up, and the area of the High Street, whose Tolbooth can be clearly seen to the right of centre, was developed. Development in Barns Road, Culzean Road and Greenside was made possible with the introduction of water under pressure. Only when the plentiful county supply was piped in were houses built up Gardenrose Path; before this Gardenrose Farm (at the top left of the picture) was supplied by a windmill pump.

First published in the United Kingdom, 2000, reprinted 2007
by Stenlake Publishing Limited, 54-58 Mill Square,
Catrine, Ayrshire, KA5 6RD
Tel: 01290 551122
www.stenlake.co.uk

ISBN 9781840331202

THE PUBLISHERS REGRET THAT THEY CANNOT SUPPLY
COPIES OF ANY PICTURES FEATURED IN THIS BOOK.

FURTHER READING

The books listed below are a sample of those used by the author during her research. None of them are available from Stenlake Publishing. Those interested in finding out more are advised to contact their local bookshop or reference library.

The Statistical Account of Scotland 1791 – 1799, Vol. VI.
The New Statistical Account of Scotland 1845, Vol. V.
The Third Statistical Account of Scotland, Ayrshire, 1951.
Ken Andrew, *Guide to the Kyle and Carrick District of Ayrshire*, 1981.
Catherine Lucy Czerkawska, *Fisherfolk of Carrick*, 1975.
Michael C. Davis, *The Castles and Mansions of Ayrshire*, 1991.
James T Gray, *Maybole, Carrick's Capital*, 1982.
Rev. R. Lawson, *Places of Interest About Maybole*, 1891.
Rev. R. Lawson, *Fifty-four Views of Carrick with Description*, 1894.
John Seymour, *Maybole, A Pictorial History*, 1982.

ACKNOWLEDGEMENTS

I would like to thank the townspeople of Maybole who willingly supplied me with information in the Bank of Scotland, the Library, the Castle, the Cassillis Hotel, the Dairy Corner, and various shops and street corners; also people of Culroy, Dunure, Maidens, Straiton, Crosshill, and Kirkmichael. I also owe a debt to the Maybole website, www.maybole.org, which contains a wealth of information and images.
I am also grateful to the following for their help: the staff of the Carnegie Library in Ayr and the Mitchell Library in Glasgow, the Turnberry Hotel, Mr Jim Grant of the Scottish Maritime Museum, Mr Robert Crawford, the Reverend Gerald Jones of Kirkmichael, and the Marchioness of Ailsa.
The publishers wish to thank Alex McGowan for providing the pictures on the front cover and pages 1, 2, 4, 5, 6, 7 (both), 8 (both), 9, 10, 11, 15, 16, 17, 18, 19, 20, 21, 22, 24, 25 (top), 28, 29, 31, 37, and 44, and Stuart Marshall for providing the picture on page 30.

Ashgrove House in Maybole, originally called Craigengillan, was built by James A. Gray, the owner of the Ladywell shoe factory. From its position at the top of Kirklandhill Path it was said that Gray could look down on the 'Bog Lum', the chimney of the Ladywell Factory. It was used in the early twentieth century as a holiday home for children from Glasgow. A housing estate was later built in the grounds.

INTRODUCTION

The first reference to Maybole appears on a charter of 1193, in which Duncan, Earl of Carrick, granted 'the lands of Meibothelbeg and Bethoc in Carric' to the monks of Melrose for the building of a church. Over the centuries 'Meibothelbeg' became 'Maybotel' and then 'Minniebole' before arriving at its modern name, which means 'the town above the mire', as it sat on a hillside above a marsh which was later drained for farming.

The domination of Carrick by the Kennedys and their chiefs, the Earls of Cassillis, ensured favoured status for Maybole and the surrounding districts where they had their residences. Robert the Bruce, whose maternal grandfather was an Earl of Carrick, spoke at Bannockburn of his 'ain men from Carrick' and this part of the country played a special part in the fight for Scotland's independence, for which Bruce had launched the first thrust at Turnberry Castle in 1307. Other Earls of Cassillis who never sat on the Scottish throne did not let this deter them from styling themselves 'Kings of Carrick', and belonging to the 'Kingdom of Carrick' was a matter of pride for the people of this district for centuries.

In 1516 King James V granted a Charter of Barony which gave Maybole its own council, which went on to administer the town for over three hundred years, and the townspeople the right to hold a market each Thursday and to have a market cross set up. As a result trade flourished and by the seventeenth century Maybole had become an important town in Ayrshire, the site of the chief court of the bailiery of Carrick where the magistrates met annually to 'fix the stent', inspect the wells, and see to other matters of town government. Also, by this time many of the lairds of North Carrick had built winter residences in the principal street of the town, which is now Abbot Street. Most of these houses had been abandoned by the end of the 1600s (one of them was converted into the Tolbooth and jail), but the town's prosperity continued, its main street becoming the High Street with the Market Cross planted firmly in the middle, and it remained the winter residence of the Earl of Cassillis whose castle stood at the foot of the High Street.

All early descriptions of the town refer to the plentiful supply of good water from its numerous wells and springs and this contributed greatly to the town's development. This healthiness of the water and the town's open and airy situation was also a reason why Maybole developed a reputation for producing townspeople of great longevity; no plague or cholera ever touched Maybole. The surrounding pastureland enabled the district to support itself and to export produce, and Carrick cattle were famous for their quality. At one time everyone in the town was connected with food production in one way or another.

By the eighteenth century most of the townspeople had turned to weaving to make their living. The men worked their own handlooms while the women and children washed, carded and spun the wool. The women also produced the celebrated Ayrshire embroidery, white figuring worked on white muslin and cotton, which started in Maybole. The weavers initially produced mainly blankets and rough cloth, but by the end of the eighteenth century cotton looms had been introduced by Irish immigrants; in 1792 two dozen out of the town's hundred or so looms were for cotton weaving, and this proportion was to increase in the next century. Pay and conditions were in the hands of the cloth agents, who supplied the wool and yarn and sold the finished product. This meant cramped conditions and miserable rates of pay for the weavers, who were often in debt to the agents, and had to buy not only their raw materials but also their household provisions at their prices. Eventually, handloom weaving could not compete with the powerlooms set up in the large industrial centres and weaving died out as a cottage industry during the nineteenth century.

Weaving was replaced by two new industries: boot and shoe making and the manufacture of agricultural implements. The former was begun in the mid-nineteenth century by shoemakers who had been making boots and shoes in their own workshops and employing others in a small way. The decline of weaving had left an existing workforce and by 1891 ten shoe factories employed 1,500 workers and sold a million pairs of boots and shoes a year through a national chain of 'Maybole Shoe Shops'. The ancillary industry of leather-tanning also prospered and was eventually concentrated in one large tannery at Ladywell which was owned by the Millar Tanning Co. Ltd. However, the end products, mainly heavy boots for agricultural use, were handmade and the advent of mechanization led to the closure of the larger factories which had not adapted.

The closure of the Ladywell factory, the town's largest, in 1907, proved a terrible blow to the town and many families emigrated to Canada. Some of the smaller factories adopted mechanized production and carried on. The First World War created demand for boots, which helped the trade, but decline set in again, hastened by the superseding of leather boots by the rubber Wellington and by punitive trade barriers erected by Ireland which was an important market. The last remaining factory, Lees & Co., was destroyed by fire in 1962, ending a hundred years of shoe production in Maybole.

The manufacture of agricultural implements also took advantage of the pool of labour left by the weaving trade and Alexander Jack set up a factory at Townhead, which continued under the name of Jack's after his death. Thomas Hunter's smaller firm merged with it, and the resulting business continued to manufacture, innovate and export to many parts of the world. After the Second World War, however, business declined and it closed down in the 1960s. By then Maybole was suffering from the disadvantages of not being close to a large centre of population or to sources of raw materials; transport costs were high and it could not compete with towns more favourably positioned.

Maybole's agricultural surroundings have always been the town's focus, although it is barely four miles from the sea. The Carrick fishing villages, strung out along the coast, have traditionally been self-sufficient communities that looked to their inland neighbour for little else than a market for their fish. Dunure and Maidens sent their produce to Maybole by pony and cart, and later by motorcycle and sidecar, and later still by van. Family ownership of boats and the need to marry a woman who had learned the skills of baiting the lines, were two factors tending to make the fishing communities close-knit. It is many years since fish were landed at either port. The small harbour at Dunure proved unsuitable for larger modern boats, and in the later twentieth century the fleet had to be berthed at Ayr or Troon. Maidens had a larger harbour, with a pier rebuilt in 1958, but the harbour silted up at the mouth and the boats had to be berthed in Ayr and Girvan.

The easy availability of transport to Ayr has changed the character of Maybole and its satellite villages during the twentieth century. Work, leisure and shopping are now more likely to be located many miles from home. The days of one or two large industries employing the bulk of the population are long gone. But many reminders of those days persist, in the buildings themselves and in the names of the streets and districts. Maybole is rich in both forms of memorial.

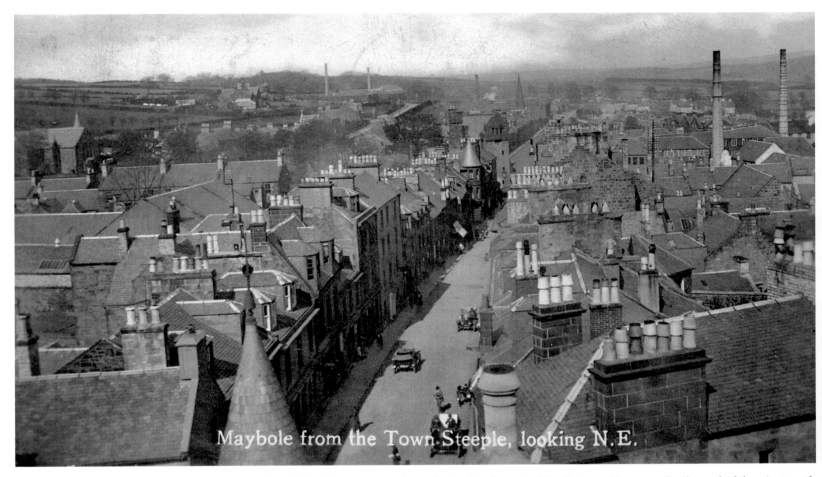

Maybole from the Town Steeple, looking N.E.

The most noticeable change in the view of Maybole from this vantage point today is the absence of the factory chimneys. By the end of the nineteenth century Maybole was a busy industrial town producing boots and shoes which were sold all over Britain, and agricultural implements which were exported throughout the world. During the first half of the twentieth century the footwear factories closed down one by one. In the eighteenth century and before, the main street of Maybole was Abbot Street, below the High Street which was at that time just a roadway between the Castle and the Tolbooth. The outbuildings of both of these spread across the road and blocked access. The High Street used to be much broader than this, before the buildings on the south side were erected in front of the older buildings, many of which still stand behind the present shops.

The house with the pillars and the gas lamp, now the premises of the Bank of Scotland, was the town house of Sir Thomas Kennedy of Culzean and later of William Niven. Niven was born in 1759, the same year as Robert Burns, and the two met as seventeen year olds in Kirkoswald and became friends; Burns visited Niven's family at the weekends and he corresponded with Niven for the rest of his life. The lives of the two men took very different paths, Niven becoming a wealthy landowner and merchant, a bailie of the town, a justice of the peace, a municipal magistrate – and a renowned miser. As the 'leader' of the town council, and the only townsman to have the vote before 1832, his authority was unchallenged within the council. An effective and capable council leader, he was feared rather than loved by the townspeople and on one occasion after an unpopular judgment from the Bench there was a riot during which the windows of his house were smashed. He died at his country estate of Kirkbride at the age of eighty-five, a very wealthy man: in the words of a local commentator 'gane, wi' the consent o' the hail parish'.

A small iron cross set into the surface of the High Street marks the site of the old town cross, or Mercat Cross, which was set up in the early sixteenth century and removed in 1773 as it was obstructing the roadway. It was from the town cross that public proclamations were made by 'tuck of drum', but in 1774 the drum was broken in a brawl and the town crier was given a handbell to ring instead. It was in the nineteenth century that the buildings on the left were erected, narrowing the street. The datestone on the building at the extreme left of the photograph reads 1876. The shop below it became Alexander McClymont's hat shop and McClymont also ran a draper's from the last shop before the break in the row. The shop before it was R. Kirkwood's bakery which had a bakehouse at the back. Another well-remembered business was P. & A. McConnell's the grocers, which occupied the premises next to the hat shop for much of the last century. Across the road, where the sheltered housing is now, was the Kings Arms.

In 1912 the old house next to the Carnegie Library was demolished, and the new Post Office was built in sandstone and granite to harmonize with the Castle across the street. This was the main post office for the district until after the First World War, when it became a sub-post office. In the early twentieth century mail was delivered three times a day on weekdays and once on Sundays. Postmen on their red bicycles with heavy mailbags on their front carriers were a familiar sight in the outlying villages. The Straiton mail was taken from here by pony and dogcart, and anyone wishing to travel to the village could get a lift in the mail gig. Maybole had had a post office from before 1837 and was the posting station halfway between Glasgow and Portpatrick, at which stage coaches stopped daily.

A view from the town hall to the Dairy Corner diagonally opposite, with the Castle in the distance. After the town cross had been removed from the middle of the street, the Dairy Corner, now restored by Historic Scotland and opened as a café under this name, was where people gathered to hear proclamations made from the town hall steps. Around the turn of the twentieth century, when this picture was taken, about 1,500 men were employed in Maybole's boot and shoe industry. They worked from six in the morning until six in the evening, with an hour off for breakfast and an hour for lunch. The shadows show this to be an evening photograph. Heading up the High Street, they may be coming from the St Cuthbert's Factory, which was opposite the Castle, and John Lees & Co.'s Townend works further down.

An account of Maybole written in the late seventeenth century describes how the town was 'beautifyed with the situation of two castles'. Maybole Castle was the town house of the Earls of Cassillis, where the family resided in winter. It was built in the early seventeenth century, or possibly slightly earlier, a period when all the local gentry had their winter residences in the town. At that time the town was graced with twenty-eight of these houses, but the only two that survive are the Castle and the Tolbooth. The Castle's little oriel window is a rare architectural gem. There is a legend that the sixth Earl of Cassillis imprisoned his wife, Lady Jean, in this tower after she tried to elope with the Gypsy Johnny Faa, and that she spent the rest of her life there weaving tapestries. The real Johnny Faa, however, predates both the Castle and the Countess.

Maybole's other surviving castle was once the town house of the Kennedys of Blairquhan, who sold it in 1674 to the Earl of Cassillis and the bailies of Maybole for the purpose of furnishing the town with 'ane sufficient tolbooth'. In the alterations to the house to make the Tolbooth, much of the building, which originally spread with its outbuildings across the High Street, was removed and a 'pyramide . . . into which they have mounted a fyne clock' was added to the top of the tower. The crenellated parapet was added in 1812 and the 'pyramide' was replaced with a larger spire, complete with iron crown and four clock faces, in the late nineteenth century. The Tolbooth served as a courthouse for the district of Carrick, with a prison cell below (described in an account of 1837 as 'a miserable place'), and when the courtroom was not in use it was let out for dances and plays. In 1887 a new town hall was built adjoining the tower, which received its new spire at this time. The Spooncreel, demolished in 1967, was so named because its shape resembled that of a spume creel, a basket for gathering seaweed.

The High Street, looking down Whitehall. Cameron's hardware shop, established in 1843 and advertised as having 'everything for the household, garden and farm', is still in business and although no longer in Cameron ownership, is run under the same name. W. McCulloch, watch and clock maker, had his business next to it, and next door to that was Henderson's bookseller and stationer. The house next to Henderson's was replaced by a red sandstone building, which for a time housed Briggs the Solicitors, and the stables beside it became the site of Cameron's garage.

Whitehall was named after the Hall of Whitefriars, which once stood approximately where the Royal Bank of Scotland is, on the extreme left of the photograph. The members of this Carmelite order wore white robes, hence their name. After the Carmelite house was demolished, the Sun Inn was built on this site. This was a coaching inn where passengers between Glasgow and Portpatrick (the main port for travel to Ireland) would break their journey. There were also two stage coaches which ran twice a week between Maybole and Ayr, and one which ran twice a week to Girvan.

By the turn of the nineteenth century the Castle was not often used by the Cassillis family and in 1805 the Earl agreed to demolish the outbuildings and offices which lay across what is now the street and allow a road to be made from the foot of the High Street to Duncanland Toll. Some years later the main part of the Castle was enlarged by the addition of the building on its right, providing offices and apartments for the factors of the estates of Culzean and Cassillis. It overlooks an attractive walled garden, the inner gates of which incorporate the headstone of the town's old Cross, carved on all four faces, with a moondial, a sundial, the date 1707 and a lion rampant, and the coat of arms of the Earl of Cassillis. The Carnegie Library on the opposite corner was built in 1905 from funds provided by the Andrew Carnegie Trust and was provided with recreation rooms for billiards and games. After being allowed to fall into disrepair, it is now the subject of restoration plans. The shop on the extreme right of the photograph was H. & T. McQuiston's, ironmonger and china merchant (established in 1878), and before that it was in a blacksmith's shop here that Thomas Hunter started his farm machinery business, which later merged with Alexander Jack's and supplied farm implements for the entire country and beyond.

The St Cuthbert's Shoe Factory was built by James Ramsay in the mid-nineteenth century. By 1883 it employed fifty-one workers and produced 550 pairs of boots and shoes a week. It was one of the businesses that failed between the two world wars. The building was then taken over as a store by the grain merchants Hutchison and McCreath (who were themselves taken over by West Cumberland Farmers), and then, in the 1960s, by McQuater Brothers for the same purpose. The building is now demolished, but the lower walls still stand. St Cuthberts Street on the left is still known as Smiddy Brae by some locals. The pump, with its gas lamp on top, was erected over an ancient well in the 1860s. Originally in the grounds of the Castle, it became known as My Lord's Well and when the Castle's outhouses were demolished in 1806, it became open to public access and the first pump was installed. The pump pictured was removed in the 1930s. The building on the right was demolished to make way for the Carnegie Library, and the Whiteside Bakery next to it was demolished in 1999.

Cassillis Road was formerly known as the New Yards as it was the site of the stack yards of the Earl of Cassillis, where the grain and straw paid as rent were stacked. Horses and carts, such as those of Burns the milkman from Crosshill, were a familiar sight in the streets of Maybole right into the 1950s. The building on the right was the St Cuthberts Inn, now the Cassillis Hotel. Next to it was Ferguson's sweet shop, and a few doors further down was the 'Low Co', the branch of the Carrick Provident Co-operative Society at this end of town. The writer of this postcard has marked a cross over 'Mr Marshall's Works', originally the Townhead Factory of Alexander Jack, farm implement makers, which was taken over by John Marshall after Jack died in 1877. It is now occupied by the International Packaging Corporation, who have been there since 1967 and specialize in making presentation cases. Near it stands the Old Parish Church, an unusual building with a distinctive stepped steeple, built in 1808.

TOWNEND BOOT & SHOE FACTORY

The Townend Factory, belonging to John Lees and Co. Ltd, was founded in 1878 by John Lees with his son John and his son-in-law, William McKellar; it opened with fifteen employees. In 1894 the firm acquired the Lorne Tannery. The heyday of boot and shoe production in Maybole, primarily concerned with the production of heavy footwear, was over by 1907, when the largest of the factories, the Ladywell, closed down. Lees and some of the other factories carried on and by 1928 Lees employed 350 people. The Second World War gave the industry a temporary boost and Lees and Co., one of only two of the businesses to survive after the war, modernized and diversified, becoming the town's only large employer of labour. It was the last of Maybole's shoe producers when the factory was destroyed by fire in June 1962.

The School Vennal led from the top of the High Street to the Ballgreen, where the town's school was situated in the seventeenth and eighteenth centuries. According to the first *Statistical Account*, published in the 1790s, this school was 'an old mean thatched house, very unsuitable to the eminent characters, which . . . have been educated in it'. School Vennal was once a busy thoroughfare with several shops and more houses than remain at present; the Shoemakers' Guild used to hold its meetings in one of them. 'Vennal' is the Scots name for lane and by the late seventeenth century there were four vennals leading off the High Street. Back Vennal has become known as John Knox Street, and Kirk Vennal as Kirkwynd. Fore Vennal (later called "Foul Vennal" in honour of its noxious open drain, and later still Post Vennal) is now Castle Street.

The oldest building in Maybole, the Collegiate Church, has for centuries been known as the Old College. It was founded in 1371 by Sir John Kennedy of Dunure 'for the purpose of celebrating daily Divine Service for the happy state of himself, his wife Mary, and their children'. It was dedicated to the Virgin Mary and the names Ladyland and Ladywell recall the connection that these places once had with the Collegiate Church. All the land on which the town is built once belonged to it, but after the Reformation of 1560 it was taken back into the possession of the family that had gifted it, which is how Maybole came to be under the superiority of the Marquis of Ailsa, a descendant of the Kennedys. In April 1563 a band of two hundred Catholics defied the Reformation Act, which made the celebration of the Mass illegal, by assembling in the chapel 'with jakkis, speris, gunnis, and other wapins' to worship. The leaders were arrested and punished. Thereafter the building fell into disrepair and was used only as a burial place for the Cassillis family and other local gentry. The Cassillis family tomb is next to the old sacristy. In 1880 the townspeople raised a public subscription to preserve the Collegiate Church and the present walls were built around it.

Town Green and Greenside pictured around 1906. The railings were removed at the time of the Second World War for the war effort. The Greenside Inn stood across the road from here. One of its regular patrons was Geordie Cunningham who used to tie up his pony and cart to the railings. One day some boys gave Geordie a fright when they untied the pony, took it into the green and tied it up there, and then took the cart apart and carried it into the green piece by piece where they reassembled it. When Geordie emerged from the Greenside Inn he had a bit more trouble than usual getting home that day! The church on the left is Kincraig Church, built in 1880. When the congregations of the two free churches, Cargill and Kincraig, amalgamated in the 1950s, it was Cargill that continued in use and Kincraig Church was sold. It was later demolished and houses were built on the site, the name Kincraig Court serving as a reminder of what once stood there.

TOWN GREEN, MAYBOLE.

The green was originally used as grazing land. In the seventeenth century it was described as 'a pleasant plott of ground, enclosed round with an earthen wall, wherein they were wont to play at football, but now at the gowffe and byasse-bowls', whence it acquired the name Ballgreen. As the School Green (named as this on the Ordnance Survey map of 1858), it was used as a playground by the children attending the parish school and also as a stance for shows at fair time. Later in the nineteenth century it was decided to lay it out with paths and plant trees and fence it in with railings. Half of the money to pay for this was raised by public subscription and it was formally opened in 1894. The old well in the green, still in use in the latter part of the nineteenth century, served many of the old houses in Ladyland Road and just beyond the flagpole can be seen the ornamental granite fountain which was raised over the well in 1881 to commemorate Thomas Dykes, factor to the Marquis of Ailsa and the first Senior Magistrate in the town. The shelter in the centre was presented by the Carrick Provident Co-operative Society in 1932 to commemorate their jubilee and since its removal a stone memorial with a plaque commemorating the same event has marked the site.

Gardenrose Path used to be known as the Near Path to distinguish it from the Far Path (or Kirklandhill Path as it is now called). Gardenrose Cottage (otherwise known as the Bumbee) stood near where the railway bridge now is in Culzean Road and gave its name both to the Farm and to Gardenrose Path leading to it. The man with the horses is cutting oats and the three women are putting the loose corn into bundles, which would be left outside to mature before being brought in. Built before 1910, the houses were the last before the town gave way to farmland until housing was built on the lands of Gardenrose Farm in 1968.

Kirkoswald Road, Maybole

Apart from the addition of a bungalow on the left hand side of the road, Kirkoswald Road is almost unchanged from this view from around 1925. On the right is a steam tractor and threshing machine in McQuater's Yard. The yard hired these out to local farms at harvest time.

Ladyland School was built in Carrick Street in response to the Education Act of 1872. Until then the town had three church schools and the Industrial School at Greenside. These were closed when the town's 850 pupils took up residence in their new building in 1875. The official opening was celebrated the following year with a procession and a day of public celebration. The school, which became known as Carrick Academy, was destroyed by fire on the night of Sunday, 1 March, 1919. The Maybole Fire Brigade was joined by the Ayr fire-fighting force, but their combined efforts failed to save any of the building, whose interior woodwork quickly caught fire, fanned by a southwesterly wind. The *Ayrshire Post* reported: 'Naturally, there was considerable excitement in the town, and until early in the morning large crowds assembled to witness the spectacle. The wind . . . made the work of the firemen at the northern end very difficult, as they were, for the most part, enveloped in thick smoke. The scene was one which will live long in the memory of those present.'

The main entrance into Maybole from the Girvan valley, the Coral Glen, seems to have got its name from a corruption of 'quarry', the activity which formed this depression in the landscape. The West Parish Church, or Glen Kirk, was built and endowed by the generosity of the Fergussons of Kilkerran in 1842. The minister of this church from 1864 until 1907 was the Reverend Roderick Lawson, a man of considerable influence in the town. The author of many books, he researched and documented the history of Maybole and surrounding villages, and collected ballads and rhymes of local interest. Much of his energy was spent in improving the town he loved: among many other things, he raised the money, much of it his own, for a new town bell for the Tolbooth. Keen to increase the town's dignity and prestige, he persuaded the council to change the names of several of the streets: thus New Yards became Cassillis Road and Smiddy Brae became St Cuthbert's Street. Many of the older inhabitants resented these changes and continued to use the old names, which must have been one of the few matters in which Reverend Lawson, accustomed to obedience from his flock, was ever defied. The church in the distance, on Allan's Hill, is Our Lady and St Cuthberts.

The Roman Catholic Church of Our Lady and St Cuthbert was built in 1877 on Allan's Hill and was designed to echo the architecture of Crossraguel Abbey. Much of the cost was met by Captain Hunter Blair. The story is told that the carved heads inside the church were made by an old itinerant mason who came by while it was being built and asked for work hewing stones. When the builders saw how skilled he was, they asked him to carve some heads for the springers of the supporting arches, and he carved portraits of the workmen, including himself. The school connected with the church was built next to it at the same time. The road below the church is Dailly Road, formerly called Mason's Row, a corruption of *Maison Dieu*. The 'house of God' referred to was a hospice or 'spittal', connected with the Old College. The inhabitants of the cottages were among those reprimanded by the council in 1792 for '[giving] lodging and entertainment to vagrants and randy beggars who go through the streets blaspheming and cursing and swearing to the disturbance of the inhabitants'. The council imposed a fine of two Scots pounds on any person giving lodgings to such 'randy beggars'.

Cargill Free Church was built in Barns Road in 1844. It was named after the covenanter Donald Cargill who preached at nearby Ladycross in May 1681, two months before he was hanged in Edinburgh. Part of the whin boulder which marked the spot of his preaching was built into one of the walls of the church. On 30 December 1906 the church was ruined by fire, which broke out in the flue of the boiler and was fanned by a strong east wind. The Maybole Fire Brigade managed to save only the belfry and the church hall and there was later an inquiry into their efficiency. It was claimed that they took half an hour to arrive and that one of the hoses was frozen. The inquiry heard that the water supply had either been poor on the night in question (ironic, for a town so full of wells) or had not been turned on properly, and that the brigade had shown a lack of discipline. The congregation rebuilt their church, but it was demolished in 1979 and houses were built on the site.

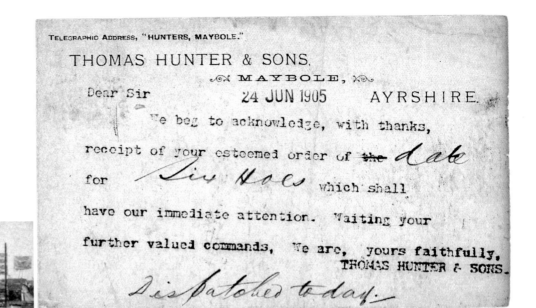

THOMAS HUNTER & SONS,

MAYBOLE,

Dear Sir   24 JUN 1905   AYRSHIRE.

We beg to acknowledge, with thanks,

receipt of your esteemed order of ~~the~~ *date*

for *Six Hoes* which shall

have our immediate attention. Waiting your

further valued commands, We are, yours faithfully,

THOMAS HUNTER & SONS.

Dispatched today.

Thomas Hunter started his business in a blacksmith's shop near the Castle and later built a factory in Alloway Road. Hunter was described by the Reverend Roderick Lawson in 1891 as one of Maybole's 'captains of industry', who manufactured 'ploughs, grubbers, turnip-sowers, etc., and these are well known from John O'Groats to Land's End. At every Agricultural Show, no figure is better known than Mr Hunter's, and no "stand" of implements more successful in securing customers or winning medals.' These cultivators, pictured inside Hunter's factory, were drawn by one or two horses, and were used to prepare the ground for sowing. In the background there are circular machines which would be powered by an engine to crush the oats before they were fed to the cattle. Hunter's became part of the larger business of Alexander Jack and Sons (taken over by John Marshall in 1877 after Alexander Jack died), and the firm went from strength to strength, exporting to many countries throughout the world. Jack's closed in the 1950s.

Lumsden House was built by Dr William McTyer and was originally named Redbrae House. The doctor had a dissecting room in an outhouse and rumour had it that local 'Burke and Hares' supplied him with subjects. One particular carrier earned the nickname 'Burke' Morrow after an incident in which his cartload of fish, parked in the yard of the public house next to the cemetery, was used as an overnight resting place by one of the inn's customers who was too drunk to travel home. The next morning, on helping himself to a herring or two, the man's hand came to rest on the foot of a corpse. By the time the town constable came to investigate the grisly report, Morrow was on his road and no dead body was found when his cart was searched. However, he had already passed Lumsden House on his way out of the town. Had the illicit cargo been offloaded at the doctor's on the way? The house was acquired by Glasgow Corporation in the twentieth century as a holiday home for the children of families who otherwise never found their way out of the city.

MAYBOLE BURGH PRIZE BAND 1904

From the early nineteenth century Maybole had a band which entertained the townspeople on summer evenings on the Town Green and on New Year's morning, when they paraded through the streets playing "A Guid New Year tae Ane and A". The band existed for well over a hundred years, initially as the Maybole Carrick Band, then the Carrick Instrumental Band, and from 1867 as the band of the Volunteers, who had been given the instruments because the town's bandsmen had given up attending practices. Around the end of the nineteenth century the instruments were returned to the council and Maybole Burgh Band came into existence. Under the bandmaster, Mr Shaw, they triumphed in many competitions, but after a decline in enthusiasm, ceased to exist in the 1950s.

The *Ayr Advertiser* of Thursday, 19 May, 1910 reported: 'In beautiful summer weather the Proclamation of the accession of His Most Gracious Majesty King George V was made in Maybole on Saturday afternoon. . . . There was a very large attendance of the general public. The town bell rang out a merry peal, and promptly to time Provost McKellar, accompanied by Bailies Millar and Fairlie, appeared outside the Council room, and the Provost read the proclamation. The bugler sounded "The Royal Salute", the Fusiliers stood at "Present Arms", and the large assembly sang "God Save the King". Three ringing cheers were given for King George.' A procession marched down to the site of the Market Cross and the proclamation was read again, and then again in front of the massed schoolchildren at the Town Green where the National Anthem was sung once more. The newspaper reported: 'All the windows along the route of march were taken advantage of by sightseers, and the glorious weather added greatly to the success of the proceedings. Flags floated mast high from the Town Buildings and flag staff on Town Green throughout the day.' This postcard was sent on 18 May, four days after the proclamation.

The view of Maybole from Dailly Road, looking across Ladywell Stadium. It was on the old pitch here, shortly before the First World War, that the Maybole team (probably the Amateurs), having entered for the Scottish Cup, found themselves drawn against Glasgow Rangers. Despite being cheered on by practically the entire town the team lost 13 – 0. Between the wars a football pitch was created at Gardenrose, but in 1945 the old pitch was completely renovated by volunteers from among the members and supporters. A clubhouse and stand were built and the 'Tacketies' moved back to take possession of the Ladywell Stadium. A junior football team was started at the same time.

The Maybole Amateurs Football Club had its greatest success during the 1935–36 season when it won the League Championship and played in the final for the Ayrshire Post trophy.
Left to right, back row : R. Cruikshank, R. Cumming, H. Houston, W. Alexander, J. Clark, A. Murdoch, R. Harvey, G. Marshall, D. Heron, T. Harris, H. Lang.
Front row: J. Crawford, A. Frew, W. Sharpe, R. McKeeman, W. McDill (Capt.), N. Hair, S. Qua.

The original tower of Cassillis, visible rising behind the later additions, dates possibly from the fourteenth century. A new stair-tower in the seventeenth century gave it an L-plan arrangement and extensive alterations to the roof and garrets were made then too. The 12th Earl of Cassillis (and the first Marquis of Ailsa), Archibald Kennedy, had the major additions built in 1831. While Cassillis House has always been in the possession of the Earls of Cassillis (the 'Kings of Carrick'), for many years Culzean Castle was their chief residence. It was David, the 7th Marquis, who made Cassillis once again the family home and carried out restoration of the older parts of the house. The tree on the left is the famous Dule (or gallows) Tree, a spreading plane, from which Johnny Faa, king of the Gypsies, is said by legend to have been hanged, while the Countess, with whom he had run off, was forced to watch. The Earl and Countess in question, however, were not contemporaries of Faa, and the tree, which was blown down in a storm of the winter of 1939–40, proved not to be of sufficient antiquity either, being only about two hundred years old.

Culroy is a hamlet west of Minishant; in the nineteenth century Minishant itself was known as Culroy while Culroy was called Upper Culroy. The Culroy Inn was frequented at that time by Dunure fishermen who came over to cut hazel wands for making creels. Bootmakers from Maybole drank there too and fights sometimes broke out between the two factions. Next to the inn is the smithy, run in the mid-nineteenth century by John Boyd, son of the proprietors of the inn. John McCall had a joiner's and wheelwright's shop on the opposite side of the road in the same period.

Dunure is the best preserved of the fishing villages on this part of the Ayrshire coast. The sheltered harbour used to be home to a sizeable fleet, but it is no longer deep enough for the keels of today's boats. The harbour, created at the beginning of the nineteenth century, was not designed with fishing in mind, but for shipping coal from a pit near Fisherton school, a venture that did not really get off the ground. The cottages were built around 1800. Many are of the but-and-ben type, with two rooms and a loft, half of which was used for storing gear and half as sleeping quarters for the boys of the family. The writer of this 1905 postcard remarked that the only two shops in the village are in this row. Both are still in use as shops: one is the white cottage second from the left and the other is the last one on the right.

A 50 metre-wide channel was cut from the deep water at Dunure Point to lead into this harbour. The lighthouse at the harbour entrance was never supplied with a light, and it must have been a difficult job to steer through the jagged rocks on either side on bad nights. On the right side of the harbour are frames for drying and cleaning the fishing nets and lines. Small open boats such as those pictured here were used for line fishing. The 'small lines' were used to catch whiting and haddock. Each line, consisting of 1,200 hooks, was baited with mussels by the womenfolk, skilled but laborious work. The men came back with their catch after four or five hours at sea and the lines, emptied of their catch, were hung on wooden poles (speets) to be dried and made ready for baiting again.

The house and shop at the end of the harbour row, pictured around 1905. Set into the wall on the right is the weather glass, a barometer which the fisherman consulted each day before setting out.

DUNURE HOUSE.   M. LEVY, AYR.

Dunure House, on the shore north of the harbour, was probably built as a residence for the factor of the Culzean or Dunure estates. The façade has a distinctive bow at the centre of the front facing the sea. A date of construction of the original house is unknown, although the bow was probably added in the early nineteenth century. A wing was added in the later nineteenth century with a gabled entrance: it is hidden behind the foliage on the right. It is possible that a house has stood on the site since the seventeenth century.

A scant four miles from Maybole, the shore (now usually called Croy shore) is reached by a road once known as the Wrack Road, after the seaweed that was gathered there to spread on the fields. Other freight was once carried on the road, for smuggling used to be part of life all along this shore. By the mid-nineteenth century Reverend George Gray, writing in the second *Statistical Account,* could say that it had all but died out, 'beyond a few casks of *Arran Water* from the opposite shores, and a little soap from Ireland'. The shore was a place of resort for the townspeople on their one day of rest, as Reverend Gray notes disapprovingly: 'few of [the population] attend any place of worship; they spend the Sabbath in wandering over the fields and on the sea shore'. The little cottage was known as Goats Green and is now unrecognizable, with a modern house constructed around it.

The bridge over the Rancleugh Burn, which empties into Culzean Bay, was constructed for the Maidens and Dunure Light Railway, a single-track line covering the nineteen and a half miles between Ayr and Girvan which was constructed between 1902 and 1906. Around the same time the Glasgow and South Western Railway Company also built the Turnberry Hotel and golf course, and it was possible to travel from Glasgow to Turnberry on the line. It was hoped that the presence of the railway would encourage development of housing on this part of the coast, but the cost of the railway proved to be out of all proportion to its use, and with the increase in road transport, passenger traffic on the line between Alloway and Turnberry stopped in 1930. For a number of years potatoes were transported on the Light Railway, but even this became unprofitable. In 1955 the line between Heads of Ayr and Turnberry was closed. Only the piers of the bridge remain now, home in recent years to a pair of peregrine falcons.

Until the middle of the last century, Maidens consisted of a number of cottages along the shore and one tenement block. The bungalows that now characterize the village were built after the First World War. Near the cottages on the left of the photograph is the place known as Wearyneuk. The story is told that when Robert the Bruce landed here to launch his attack on Turnberry Castle further down the coast, he was told that what he had taken for landing fires were not signals, but whins which had caught fire. A frustrated Bruce said: 'This is a weary neuk to land in.'

The Knowe, Maidens.

The harbour of Maidens, having become silted up, was completely reconstructed in 1958 as a place for boats engaged in seine and ring fishing. Less than twenty years later, however, it had silted up at the mouth again, and Maidens boats had to be berthed at Ayr and Girvan. Ring netting was the method used to catch herring in the days when they were plentiful off the Scottish coast. The net was worked by a pair of boats, encircling the shoal of herring. The Carrick fishermen worked in the Firth of Clyde, moving up to the North West coast towards the end of the year and fishing the Isle of Man in summer. The herring were landed fresh every day at whichever port was nearest. The herring fishing lasted for nine months of the year and white fishing occupied the other three.

TURNBERRY HOTEL, AYRSHIRE. THE PROPERTY OF THE G. & S. W. RY CO. TO BE OPENED IN 1905.

It was the 3rd Marquis of Ailsa, landowner, golfer and director of the Glasgow and South Western Railway Company, who initiated golfing at Turnberry. In 1901 he commissioned Willie Fernie, the professional at the Troon Golf Club, to lay out a course and the following year Turnberry Golf Club was founded. The golfing facilities were taken over by the Glasgow and South Western Railway Company, and a light railway, the Dunure and Maidens Light Railway, was built from Ayr to Girvan. At Turnberry a hundred-bedroom luxury hotel was designed (by James Millar, who designed the Glasgow Exhibition of 1901), connected by a covered way to the station, to accommodate the golfing fraternity. Both railway and hotel were opened on 17 May, 1906. The hotel boasted the most modern and luxurious conveniences, including electric lifts, and 'suites of bathrooms with plunge baths, sprays, showers and waves, and supplied with hot and cold, fresh and salt water'. A second golf course was opened in 1909.

GOLF HOUSE, TURNBERRY

After the British Open of 1977 the clubhouse was extended with a restaurant, bar and six extra rooms, and became known as the Dormie House. It was demolished in 1993, when the new clubhouse was built nearby. During both world wars the golf courses at Turnberry were flattened and made into an airfield, and the hotel became a hospital. Twice they were restored: the damage done in the Second World War was so extensive, with fairways buried under two feet of concrete, that many thought that golfing at Turnberry was finished. Thousands of tons of soil were moved, the courses were redesigned, and the new courses were opened in 1950 and 1954 respectively.

7TH GREEN & TEE "BRUCES CASTLE"

From the seventh green can be seen Turnberry Castle, thought to be the birthplace of Robert the Bruce, who inherited the Earldom of Carrick through his mother Marjory. It was here that the Scottish nobles met in 1286 to plan their promotion of Bruce's claim to the Scottish throne. In 1307 Bruce led an assault on the castle to oust the English who had taken possession of it. It was partly successful, and ultimately led to the withdrawal of the intruders, a series of events which culminated in the Battle of Bannockburn. The lighthouse was built in the castle courtyard in 1874.

Turnberry Post Office, next to the hotel, was struck by lightning during an exceptionally severe thunderstorm on the evening of 16 January, 1909. According to a report in the *Ayr Advertiser*, the postmaster, Mr Ross, was reading in the kitchen 'when . . . he heard a dreadful roar, and was immediately thrown violently to the other side of the room. Picking himself up, the next thing he recollected was the roof falling in. Forcing a passage to the hall of the house, he heard piercing shrieks coming from the bedrooms where his sisters were, and after extricating the invalid [one of the sisters was confined to bed], placed her on his shoulders, and retraced his steps . . . All were much overcome with the fumes of sulphur.' Postcards were meant to be topical in those days: this one was sent less than two weeks after the incident.

STRAITON VILLAGE

Straiton's main street still has its two rows of cottages, which were laid out by Thomas, 9th Earl of Cassillis in the 1760s. The Black Bull Inn, on the right, has the date 1763 inscribed on the wall, with the armorial bearings of the Whiteford family and the heads of Tam O'Shanter and Souter Johnnie. The Whitefords were the predecessors of the Hunter Blairs of the Blairqhuan estate. A memorial to Lt. Col. James Hunter Blair, killed at Inkerman in the Crimea in 1854, was erected on Bennan Hill, but after being struck by lightning, was moved to its present site of Craigengower, where it can be seen in the background right of the picture. In 1837 the village had two schools, a parish library, two Sabbath schools and four public houses. Between 1792 and 1837 the parish had undergone a substantial rise in population and had acquired improved roads and new houses.

Fresh Arrival at Kirkmichael House Convalescent Home, by Maybole.

Parts of Kirkmichael House are said to date back to the early fifteenth century and it was owned by the Kennedy family. In 1920 they sold it to the Ayrshire District Welfare Committee who converted it into a convalescent home for miners. This opened in 1923 and was funded by the Miners' Welfare Fund which was run jointly by the Ayrshire Coalowners' Association and the Ayrshire Miners' Union. Under the terms of the Mining Industry Act of 1920, the coalowners contributed a penny per ton and the miners a penny a week. Ayrshire was the first county to put the welfare scheme into operation and the purchase of the house was suggested by James Baird Thorneycroft of William Baird and Company (who left a legacy of £1,000). It could accommodate up to a hundred miners and staff and had electricity, hot water, bathrooms, a library, billiard room, smoking and recreation rooms, and an estate with loch and woodlands. In 1956 the home was closed (by then it was dubbed 'the old men's home') and replaced by one in Troon, more popular with the younger miners. The house was then taken over by Ayrshire Education Committee and became a home for 'maladjusted children'. It has been in private ownership from the mid-1990s.

McCOSH CLUB. KIRKMICHAEL.

The McCosh Hall, the gift of Dr John McCosh, native of Kirkmichael and Surgeon to the 31st Regiment of Bengal Native Infantry, was opened on 13 December 1899. The President, Frederick Shaw Kennedy, entertained the members to a dinner, followed by a concert and dance. Mrs Kennedy performed the official opening and gave a speech in which she said that Dr McCosh had bequeathed the means to build the club, 'where the men of Kirkmichael might spend their leisure hours happily in congenial recreations, and . . . where social gatherings could be held, and amusements provided in which the whole village could participate'.

DALHOWAN STREET, CROSSHILL, MAYBOLE

J.HUNTER, AYR

Crosshill, south of the River Girvan, was a weaving village, which came into existence in the late eighteenth or early nineteenth century to supply cloth to the Glasgow merchants who put out the spun yarn to the weavers. The women of the village also supplied fine Ayrshire needlework. The original village was strung out in a long line along Dalhowan Street and King Street. Most of the cottages had two rooms, one of which was occupied by the handloom. This view, very little changed today, is taken from the last cottage in the row at the south end of the village, number 91. In the middle ground there is a standpipe: originally these cottages did not have internal water supplies. One or two defunct standpipes can still be seen.